ART AND ENTERTAINMENT IN ANCIENT AFRICA

Ancient History Books for Kids Grade 4 Children's Ancient History

BABY PROFESSOR
EDUCATION KIDS

Speedy Publishing LLC

40 E. Main St. #1156

Newark, DE 19711

www.speedypublishing.com

Copyright 2017

In this book, we're going to talk about art and entertainment in Ancient Africa. So, let's get right to it!

Africa is a huge continent. Civilization began in Africa, and throughout the centuries, empires have started, grown very populated, and then been overthrown by other kingdoms or by other countries. Each civilization has had its own customs, beliefs, and native art.

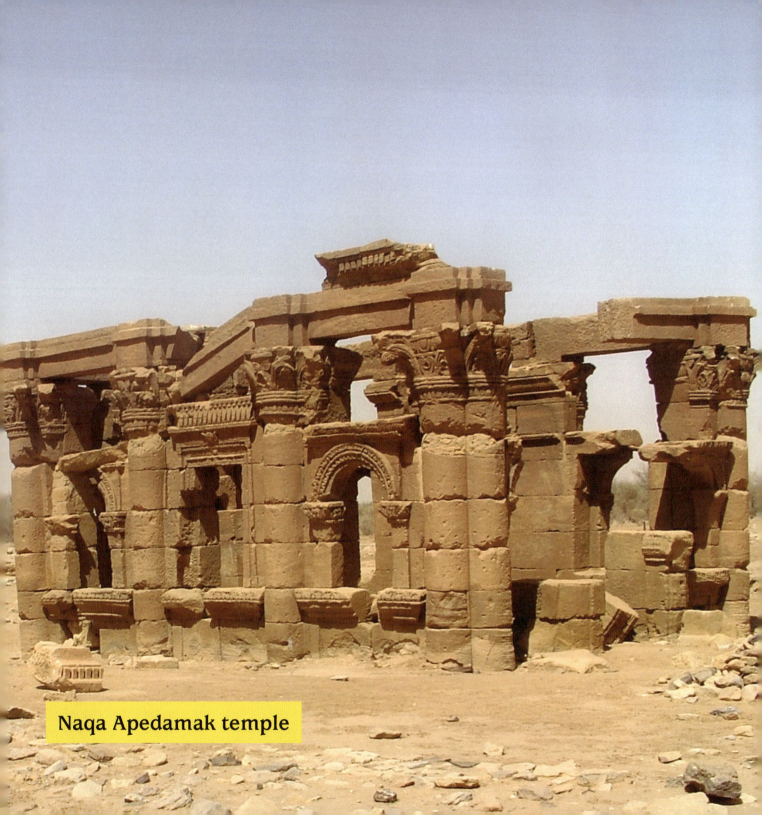

Naqa Apedamak temple

ART WAS DIFFERENT IN EACH REGION

The art of Africa varies by region and was influenced by people from foreign lands who conquered the ancient civilizations. For example, the African art in the north part of Africa was transformed because of the Muslim culture after the Arabs conquered that region.

The Christian Europeans who settled in Ethiopia and the Horn of Africa influenced the art produced in those regions. The art of the ancient civilization of Egypt is a completely different style that is uniquely Egyptian and not found anywhere else. However, when we think of "African art" we often think of masks and sculptures.

African masks

African art

This is the art of the native tribes of Africa. This type of art was primarily created by the people who lived south of the vast Sahara Desert.

WHAT MATERIALS WERE USED TO CREATE ANCIENT AFRICAN ART?

Many pieces of ancient African art were created using wood and wood doesn't survive well over a long period of time unless it becomes fossilized. Pieces of art created with metals, such as bronze or iron, have survived. Many ceramic and ivory pieces have survived from ancient times as well.

Saharan rock art

ANCIENT ROCK PAINTINGS

Scattered throughout the countryside of the country of Namibia, there are ancient rock paintings. These "paintings" are etched into the rock as well as painted and show scenes with people and animals. Archaeologists believe they are some of the oldest art ever created since they date back 20,000 years.

ART IN THREE DIMENSIONS

One of the characteristics of ancient African art is that it was often three-dimensional. Instead of two-dimensional flat drawings or paintings, African artists preferred the realism of three-dimensional sculptures, pottery, masks, and jewelry.

African Sculpture

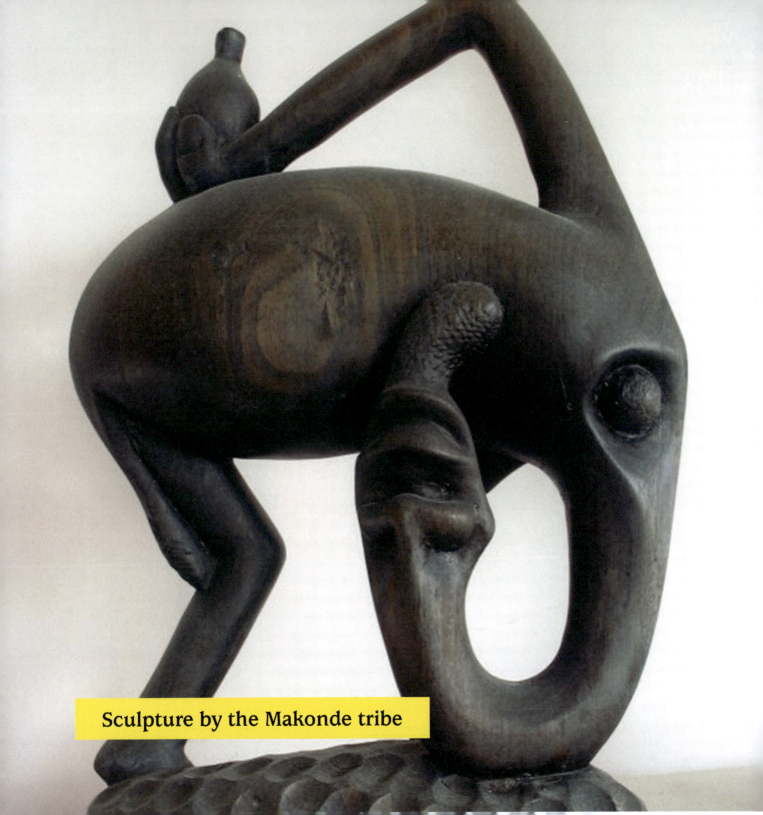

Sculpture by the Makonde tribe

Sculpture

Sculpture was used frequently in ancient African art and often had religious significance. People and animals were both depicted in sculpture. Artists used a variety of materials to create these works of art. Wood was often used and painted with bright colors. They also used bronze as well as terracotta. Ivory was taken from the tusks of elephants and rhinos to make sculptures as well.

Sometimes smaller patterns within a sculpture or parts of a sculpture were repeated again at a larger size within the same sculpture. This artistic technique is known as "nonlinear scaling."

Sculpture of the Ife civilization

African Wood Mask

Masks

Tribal masks have always been an important type of African art. Used with dance and music, masks were created to perform religious rituals and to tell stories. Some artists would go through a purification process and make offerings to ancestors before carving a ceremonial mask.

Masks were often made with wood and were decorated with colorful paint as well as jewels, animal fur, and sometimes pieces of ivory. Many masks were faces of animals and they symbolized the animals' spirits during religious rituals.

African Jewelries

Jewelry

Jewelry was one way that people from ancient Africa displayed their position in society as well as their level of wealth. Most jewelry was made from common items they were able to find such as shells, rocks, and beads. Jewelry for the wealthy was made with gold and gems. Necklaces, bracelets, and earrings sometimes identified a particular tribe.

Pottery

Ceramic materials were used to create the cooking pots to prepare food and the bowls used for serving. Some pottery was used for art and decoration and these items were painted with detailed designs.

THE GRIOT AS HISTORIAN

Before written language, there was no way to retain the history of a village except through oral storytelling. Griots were good at memorizing. Since there was no written language, everything they knew was held within their memories.

This was one of the reasons that repetition was important in oral storytelling. Each time the griot told a story, it became easier and easier to remember. The stories were probably embellished, exaggerated, and made more entertaining with each passing generation.

THE HUMAN FORM

Much of ancient African art revolves around representations of the human form. However, the forms shown were not always true to life. Different features were often exaggerated and sometimes features were left out altogether. Humans and animals were combined into unique and unusual shapes. This abstract representation of people and animals eventually influenced art in Europe during the evolution of modern art.

ENTERTAINMENT IN ANCIENT AFRICA

An important role in ancient African culture was the role of griot. Griots told stories and were entertainers. Before the advent of written language, storytellers were important to the culture of every village. In fact, the role was so important that most villages had one man who was a full-time griot. Larger cities had more than one griot.

Griots

THE GRIOT AS STORYTELLER

The griot actually had many roles within the function of a storyteller. He would entertain the village by telling and retelling religious and mythical stories about the region's gods, animal spirits, and ancestors. Sometimes the griot's stories would center around the lives or adventures of famous leaders or soldiers.

Tales of epic past battles and events were told in an entertaining style so that the villagers could relive these scenes from the village's past. Other stories were designed to help children understand the difference between good and evil. They were moral lessons so that people would respect each other and be kind to one another. Teaching good character traits helped to make the village stronger and a better community.

North African pottery

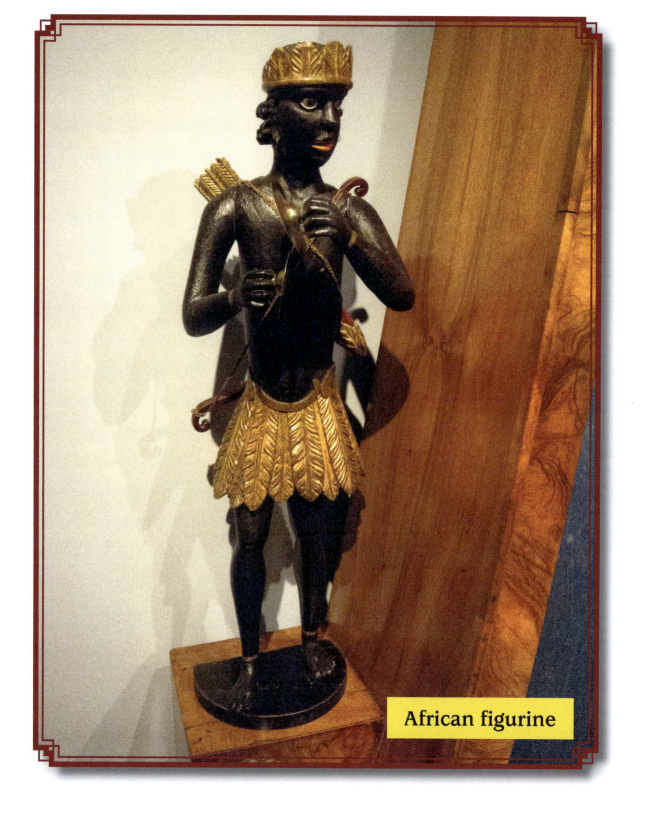

African figurine

A Griot playing a Ngoni

The village's griot knew when each child had been born and when each couple had been married. Important events regarding the weather, such as times when the rains came or when there were droughts, were remembered by them. They kept track of all the important events and life transitions within the village.

They were the keepers of the important stories and events that were critical to the village's history as well as identity. These important stories became part of the village's entertainment and cultural core for generation after generation as the griots passed them down.

Although the role of griots was very important, they were not considered to be upper class. However, they were well respected by the villagers. Sometimes they were feared because their storytelling powers were considered magical. Griots were sometimes the most masterful speakers within their villages so when negotiations with other villages were needed, the griots frequently were mediators in disputes.

THE GRIOT AS MUSICIAN

The griot didn't just speak the words of a story for entertainment. Sometimes, stories were sung and music was played to emphasize important parts of a particular story. In a village with more than one griot, each one may have specialized in one type of musical instrument.

Ancient musical instruments

There were three types of instruments that were very popular with griots in ancient Africa.

The Balafon

The balafon is a large instrument that is something like a xylophone. It is made up of gourds and wood. Its twenty-seven keys are struck with a mallet made out of rubber or wood. Balafons have been in existence since the 1300s. A balafon has a high-pitched resonant sound that's very distinctive. It was thought that the balafon had magical powers.

Balafon

African musician playing Kora

The Kora

A calabash, which is a very large squash, was cut in half to make a kora. A cow skin was used to cover the calabash and a long neck of hardwood was attached to it. A kora has strings similar to a harp, but it also has characteristics of a lute, which is another type of stringed instrument. The kora has twenty-one strings. Eleven of the strings are played by the musician's left hand and ten of the strings are played by the right hand.

The Ngoni

Like the kora, the ngoni is also a stringed instrument. The body of the instrument is made with a piece of wood that has been hollowed out. The opening is covered with animal skin. The ngoni only has five or six strings compared to the twenty-one strings of the kora. Some historians believe that when slaves from West Africa came to the Americas, their ngoni instruments were the beginnings of the banjo.

Ngoni

DANCE AND MUSIC IN ANCIENT AFRICA

In addition to listening to the stories and music performed the griots, ancient tribes in Africa enjoyed dancing in groups to music and drumbeats. The villagers used dance and music to chase evil spirits away and to pay their respects to good spirits as well as their ancestors. The beat of the drums in tribal music echoed the heartbeats of the villagers. The rhythm of dance, music, songs, and chanting created a community spirit of joy within the village.

Awesome! Now you know more about art and entertainment in Ancient Africa. You can find more Ancient History books from Baby Professor by searching the website of your favorite book retailer.

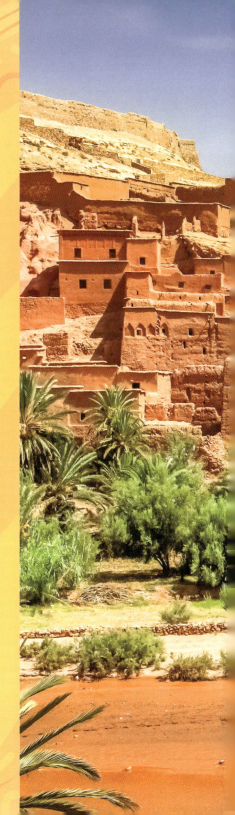

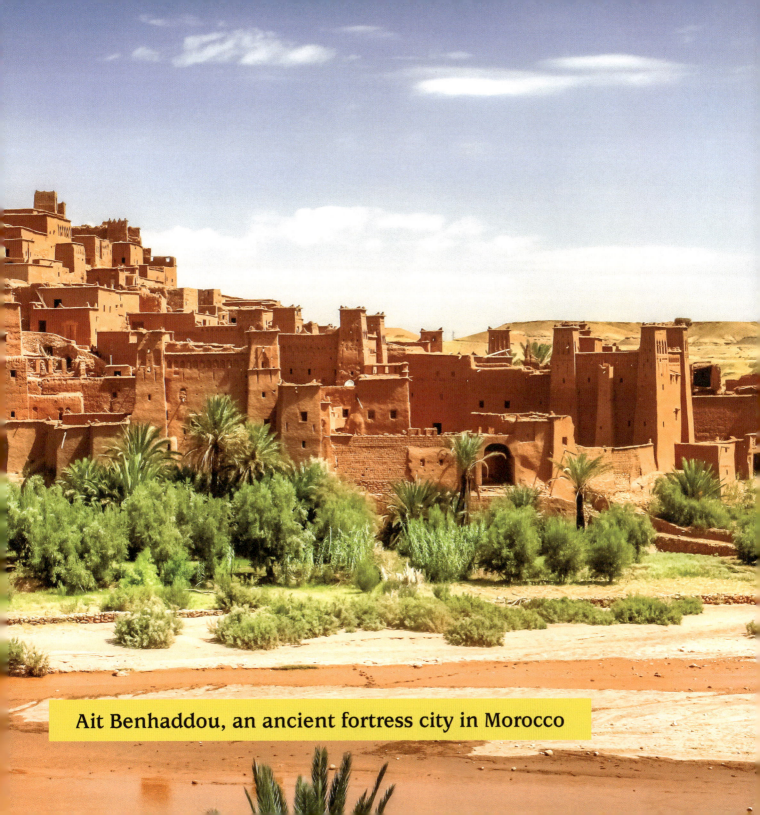

Ait Benhaddou, an ancient fortress city in Morocco

Visit

BABY PROFESSOR
EDUCATION KIDS

www.BabyProfessorBooks.com

to download Free Baby Professor eBooks
and view our catalog of new and exciting
Children's Books

Printed in Great Britain
by Amazon